AFRIKANS RECLAIM YOUR NAMES, IDENTITY AND DIGNITY.

AFRIKANS RECLAIM YOUR NAMES, IDENTITY AND DIGNITY

By Abolade Nkosi Tayo

Cover Art by Abolade Nkosi Tayo

Contents

FOREWORD

This is an expansion of a small booklet I wrote a few years ago, this became necessary, as I have acquired more knowledge, have greater experience, clearer insight and a better understanding why even conscious Afrikans still refuse to reclaim their names.

Some have even come to accept the misnomer "THIRD WORLD PEOPLE" How can we be "Third World People?" We are the Original People, which had the earliest most advanced civilization, complete with reasonable practical laws, which not only governed the people, but provided for them in a humane way.

When a great man such as Marcus Garvey says "Up you mighty race, you can accomplish what you will," I often wonder how many of us truly grasp the magnitude of such a positive statement, such a fact, such a reality, as it should wake up any sleeping Afrikan from the slumber of indifference and ignorance, yes we can accomplish what we will, if we start to love each other, educate each other, support all black owned businesses, set good examples for the younger ones, so that they do not get hooked on alcohol, cigarettes, cigars, crack, heroin etc., set examples of good family relations, a husband and wife relationship, set good examples, be a good father, a good mother, a good uncle, a good aunt, a good neighbour, be real not fake, practice what you teach, your way of life is the best demonstration of who you are.

You must be positive as that will be your projection, don't use abusive language period, I see and hear black people cursing their children, being intolerant to them, venting their rage on these small children, remember that these very children are the results of seeds planted, and they are like young trees, if they are not nurtured properly, their chances of growing up well mannered, positive, productive and being an excellent role model may be diminished, I would not say totally negated, as a few who grew up under those same debilitating circumstances, have emerged as really good people by the mercy of the Almighty Creator.

But just imagine if those same children had good upbringing by positive parents, how much easier it would have been for them to accomplish what they did. I am a published Author and what gives me great joy and happiness are the positive comments my readers give me, after reading my books, that makes me feel much better than the monetary profit. Just the knowledge that my books had such positive impacts, that is really hard to describe. You may not be an Author, but you can make positive contributions in so many ways, just look around you, you can begin from your own home and let it flow out, it gets easier after you make that first step, try it and if you have already made that first step, you are on the right track, just continue.

Another myth is not recognizing the Great Afrikans in History, a lot of Historians write a lot of untruths, take a few examples they say that Hippocrates is "THE FATHER OF MEDICINE", which is incorrect and very misleading, but if you tell a lie so many times it sounds like the truth. The truth is that "IMHOTEP IS THE FATHER OF MEDICINE" he lived over two thousand years before Hippocrates and he was a successful practicing Doctor, Surgeon and Medical Expert, by the way he was the Master Architect also. The Egyptians(Afrikans) taught the Greeks, as many of their Scholars and learned men went to Egyptian Learning Institutions, get a copy of Stolen Legacy by George M. James and read it, you will be amazed.

Look at another glaring nonsensical piece of Historical misinformation Christopher Columbus discovery of the New World, just plain lies, what he did was introduce colonization to the New World on behalf of the European Oppressors of that age. The truth is Afrikans have been to the New World centuries before Columbus, but their visits were friendly, they never oppressed the natives, they never enslaved them, they did not claim to be discoverers on behalf of Afrika, as they were just friendly visitors without any hidden agenda.If Columbus existed today, he would be called a Terrorist, as he not only terrorised the natives, but also oppressed them, yet still so much praise is given to him. Take time out to educate your children, let them know what is TRUTHFUL and what is FALSEHOOD, they will thank you in the long term, take time to do it, you will be happy.

CHAPTER 1

AFRIKANS WHO ARE THEY?

You must have heard the old beaten argument that, "I am not an Afrikan, I am a negro, I was not born in Afrika, so how can you say that I am an Afrikan?

I am an American, I am a West Indian, I am British, etc.,

I can go on and on with those oft repeated nonsense, as I have been hearing them since I was a child and I still hear them everyday.

Let's analyse them one by one, all the so-called objections.

1. I am not an Afrikan, I am a negro, I was not born in Afrika.

Okay, so you say you are a negro, which I will easily disprove right now. I want you to tell me which continent negroes come from, you tell me which language is negro language, what is negro culture and what is a negro name?

Before I disprove the fallacy of you being a negro, I will make just three references.

1. EUROPEANS are Europeans, even though they were born in China, or wherever, they are still just Europeans with designations of which European countries their ancestors originated, nothing more, nothing less.

2. CHINESE are Chinese even if they were born in Afrika, Europe, Australia or China, they are Chinese nothing more, nothing less.

3. INDIANS (East) are Indians, whether they were born in India, China, Europe, Afrika, the Caribbean or anywhere else, they are still Indians.

Now that I have made my three references, I will elaborate, Europeans have a language and many dialects, one of them is English, they have their country of origin, and their culture.

Chinese have a language and many dialects, they have their country of origin, and their culture.

Indians (East) have a language, and many dialects, they have their country of origin and their culture.

Now let us turn to the Afrikans, whether you were born in Afrika, the Caribbean, the U.S.A., Europe, Russia, Asia, India or Spain, you are only an Afrikan, nothing more, nothing less, you have your country of origin, AFRIKA, your language and dialects, and your culture, with sub designations such as Egyptian, Aethiopian, Sudanese, Zulu etc.' but collectively AFRIKANS, now let me ask you negroes, what is the "Negro Language" where is the so-called "Negro-Land" of origin, what are "Negro Foods" and what is "Negro Culture?"

You see what I mean, you can't answer those questions as the negro is only the imagination of the slave master in a bygone era, it is the actual ignoring of an entire people, culture, language, dialects etc., by assigning them to nonentity, nothingness, as before slavery there were no negroes, so after slavery how can you accept the fallacy that you are a negro, the whole answer to the question of "Negro", is in the mind of the colonial slave masters who through violence and cruelty forcefully made our ancestors accept the "Negro Myth", so why in this day and age with volumes upon volumes of reliable documented facts, you still want to cling to a mythology, why?

In the past your ancestors were brutalized to submit to the mythology of being negroes, and now you are holding on to it so tenaciously as though your very existence depended on it.

Let me quote some old, oft repeated statements and facts, "if a dog gives birth in an oven that does not make the offsprings bread, or a cat gives birth in a candy factory, does not make the offsprings candies, so how come this is applicable to animals and all other people, except the Afrikans, why us?

Now look at the stupidity, and the paradox of you accepting the misnomer "Negro", the same Europeans who called you negro, have greater respect for animals and insects, as a Doberman born in China, Europe, America, The Caribbean etc., is still only a Doberman, a Persian cat born in U.S.A., China, England, etc., is still only a Persian cat, and last but not the least, the Afrikan Bees, whether born in Brazil, the U.S.A., or Trinidad are still only Afrikan Bees or sometimes called Afrikanised Bees, how come, why double standards? Are animals and insects more important than a whole race of people?

You may argue that negro means black, but some of the blackest people I have ever seen come from India and they are never called negroes, although they be very black in complexion, why the double standards?

Any Afrikan who proudly calls himself negro in this day and age is not only sleeping, but DEAD.

Let me recapitulate, lest you fail to grasp the stark reality.

1. Chinese, land of origin is China, they have Chinese culture, Chinese names, Chinese language, and Chinese dialects, Chinese history, great Chinese male and female, Chinese food and regardless of where they were born, they look Chinese and they are Chinese.
2. Indians (East), land of origin is India, they have Indian culture, Indian names, Indian language, many Indian dialects, Indian

history, great Indians male and female, Indian food, and regardless of where they were born, they look Indian as they are Indians.

3. Europeans, land of origin Europe, they have European culture, European names, European language, many European dialects (English is one of them), European history, great Europeans male and female, even their comic books have European characters, such as Batman, Phantom, Mandrake, Spiderman, even Superman has assumed a European identity (Clark Kent), and he looks so European that no one even suspects that he is an alien, European gods, the white Jesus, Mary, Peter, Paul, Joseph etc., all as white as they could be, they have European food, and regardless of where they were born they look European, as they are Europeans.

4. Afrikans, land of origin Afrika, they have Afrikan culture, Afrikan language, many Afrikan dialects, Afrikan history, great Afrikans male and female, Afrikan food and regardless of where and when (eg. Slavery) they were born, they look Afrikan as they are Afrikan.

So you have no excuse now to accept the degrading, stupid misnomer of you being a negro, if after reading all this you are still convinced that you are a negro, then I am really sorry for you as you are not sleeping, but brain dead.

CHAPTER 2

HOW WE LOST OUR ORIGINAL NAMES

When you hear the name John Thomas, or Thomas Williams etc., you immediately conjure up a European picture, especially if you have not seen the person before and realize that he was not European.

It was no mistake, this was the design of the slave masters (physical), to make sure his names live on, by brutally taking away the Afrikan names from our ancestors, and forcefully giving them his (European) names the highest high in those names for the slaves were, that they were the property of the slave master whose name they carried, now in this day and age a worst form of slavery have taken deep roots into our very being, this time it is MENTAL, which is even more damaging than the physical slave master, but you love the mental slave master, this time around, we forcefully defend the keeping of those European names, even though some of them have not only bad meanings, but absurd meanings as well.

You see names are more important than you perceive, we are told in the Bible that the Creator changed names examples, Abram to Abraham, Jacob to Israel, and certain children were given names before their births, in this category we have John the Baptizer, Moses, Jesus (Yahshua) (pbut), so if names were not very important, then why the name changing and the commands to name certain children specific names, why?

If you hear Sun Lee, Yamamoto, Mahatma Gandhi, Gorbachev etc., you know for sure by the names, the nationality of the persons, as follows Chinese, Japanese, Indian, Russian etc., when you hear names like Abolade, Nilaja, Ayodele, Dara, Jomo, Alafia, Nzingha, Monifa, Abiola, Mansa, Imhotep etc., you know that they are our beautiful meaningful Afrikan names.

The names are not just important, but very important and very necessary, if they were not, the slave masters would never bother to change our original names, he would have just left us with our beautiful meaningful Afrikan names but they knowing the damage they could do to a whole nation, they stole our names, our nationality, our language, and our dignity, by erasing our original names and giving us their names ,so that they will live into posterity.

I am not advocating hate, as I am not on that track, what I am saying is that since the physical (material) chains have been taken off, it's high time that we could take off the mental and cultural chains which have proven to be the harder chains to be broken, than the iron shackles of the past.

Look around you and see the damage that European culture is doing to our children, our brothers, our sisters, our parents, our elders see them light up cigarette after cigarette with pride even though it has been proven to cause lung cancer, emphysema, shortness of breath, stink breath, discolouring of the teeth, finger nails, eyes, damage to the liver and other vital organs, those who are wise enough not to smoke, still have to inhale the death and sickness producing smoke of cigarettes, where is the love, where is the intelligence, is European culture so important to us that we MUST PROPAGATE it even at the expense of making ourselves and others sick, killing ourselves , our loved ones and people who inhale the poisonous smoke from our stupid actions of smoking cigarettes, cigars and pipes?

Afrikan names are so beautiful, and meaningful that it is only fair and right that we should give our children back their cultural names and you should begin with yourself.

Don't be arrogant and say that this is modern times, and a name is not so important, if that is true, how come the Europeans still give their children European names, the Indians, Indian names, the Chinese, Chinese names etc., and this is modern times.

Why make yourself the exception, why? You must have your own family names, why hold on to names that have no positive meanings or ancestral roots why?

Remember that you can peacefully and legally reclaim your name, at this point I must congratulate, all those brave, conscious and determined brothers and sisters, who have not only reclaimed their names, but are now raising a generation of children, who were given their rightful names at birth, keep it up you brave brothers and sisters, keep it up.

CHAPTER 3

ARE AFRIKAN NAMES IMPORTANT?

The answer to the title of this chapter is a loud YES, Afrikan names are very important to Afrikans born in Afrika and elsewhere, they are not only important but necessary. Let us go back to the time our ancestors were enslaved, if Afrikan names were not important to us, why did the slave makers insist that our names be changed, even going so far as to killing some of our ancestors who resisted, they maimed some and tortured some, you tell me, what was the urgency in taking away our original names, what was so important that they forcefully imposed their names on our ancestors.

The names were forced on our ancestors, just as cows are branded, it simply meant that all enslaved Afrikans were branded with the slave makers' names, signifying that they were their property, just like a cow, a horse, a goat, a sheep, a chicken etc.

There was no honor in carrying those names then, and none now, you can't trace your ancestry to a European further than the enslavement of Afrikans, so your history ends there, as your European names will take you to Europe instead of Afrika, so your present European names lead you to NO-WHERE, that's exactly what the slave makers planned to uproot you, to severe you from your roots, leave you rootless.

Here I will make a point and next show you where I stand with Afrikan names.

Right now you have Afrikans born in Afrika and elsewhere with European names from all over Europe, some have English names mixed with Dutch, Spanish, French, Russian, German and a host of bad meaning names, and a lot of foolish meaningless names were given to them (Afrikans), we have names like Willie, Lynch, Edward, George, Thomas, Garth, Franz, Luis, Louis, Charles, Audrey, Cecil, Cecilia, Macaulay, Anthony, Washington, Lincoln etc., no thought is given to combinations, or country of origin etc.

I often wonder how many Afrikans in this day and age could carry a name such as Lynch, the word Lynching was coined after the bearer of that name, who was European, and those Lynched were Afrikans, you should read the "INFAMOUS WILLIE LYNCH LETTER".

In fact, Lynching was coined after Captain Williams Lynch (1742-1820) so why should any sane Afrikan want to trace his ancestry to William Lynch a murderer, sadist and slave maker, why? And not only Lynch but a host of others which lead to persons who enslaved black people, tortured them, murdered them, raped them, demoralized them, oppressed them, frustrated them, what pride is there in this kind of ancestry?

What sane reason could any black person have for perpetuating these names, they are not your names, as originally your names were taken from you, what you have is a substitute, a poor substitute at that, it's like someone taking a gold bar from you at gunpoint, then giving you an aluminium bar and you are cherishing this junk, and then passing it on to your children, this is utter madness, madness, madness and more madness.

STOP THIS MADNESS NOW!

This is my stand on Afrikan names, we have been uprooted from all over Afrika, and also enslaved in some parts of Afrika, so my concern is not where or which part of Afrika your Afrikan names come from, but look at their meanings and pronunciation, right now you have stupid names from all over Europe, so what harm can there be if we have "Beautiful, Meaningful names from all over Afrika", this is why I have deviated from placing names of countries next to the names in chapter 9 of this book, right now, that is not necessary, don't help them fragmentise Afrika, Afrika is One Afrika.

1. Why rush to change my European names? For starters, you are not European, and you have no obligation to propagate those names, remember how our ancestors originally got those names, why honor William Lynch and those other slave makers, why?

2. Why can't I keep my "nice" European names, I have lived with these names for so long?

Who told you that a European name is nicer than an Afrikan name, what about your ancestors who were forcefully taken from Afrika, they lived a long time (centuries) with their original names, which the slave master forcefully took from them, why didn't he leave them with their nice Afrikan names which they lived so long with, why?

1. Won't that cause confusion, how would I identify with my father, grandfather, great grandfather, if I change my name?

The confusion was already caused over 400 years ago, your duty now is to end that confusion, by reclaiming your names and giving your children Afrikan names, that is the beginning of getting back on track, that is the beginning of sorting out the confusion, let me give you a living example, I have a friend whose name is Charles Bush, but what relationship is he to George Bush ex-president of the U.S.A., the answer is none, Charles Bush is black, George Bush is white, the best connection here is that George Bush's ancestors in the far past, may have been the owners of Charles Bush's ancestors, that's it, no kinship, no relationship, you see what I mean.

1. Why bother, why give yourself all that trouble?

What trouble, is it trouble for the first time in your life to have your own names, names which your ancestors bore, before slavery, is that trouble?

It should be a labor of love and dignity, not trouble.

You would actually be able to start your line with an Afrikan name, and your family (offspring) would be bearing your name, and they would have Afrikan names, this is a start, that would be in the right direction, just as the slave masters long term plan worked, we must make sure it only worked for a limited time, by reclaiming our names and perpetuating ourselves, by way of our names, thus identifying as who we are.

Reference

Chapter 3

1. The Random House Dictionary page 536

CHAPTER 4

WHY WE SHOULD RECLAIM OUR NAMES

Before I get into the subject, I must stress, that there will be some repetition, as Afrikan Culture cannot be dissected, example; in ancient Afrikan civilization people would be working in the fields singing and some of their working movements would be done in dancelike movements, so we had here

1. Work
2. Song
3. Dance

Another example Afrikan Martial Arts (Ancient & Modern) employed Martial Training, dancelike movements, and drumming, so we had (and still have)

1. Martial (Warlike) Training
2. Dance
3. Music(Drumming)

And I could go on and on, we do not divide, all are interwoven, it is the total sum, not the parts.

The above references were made to drive home the points as to why we should reclaim our names, we have to be total, complete, it is not good enough for John Thomas to realize that he is Afrikan, he must go another step further, he should reclaim his name, then respectfully, consciously, progressively, culturally carry his name, he should be proud every time his name is mentioned whether it be as a good son, a good father, a good brother, or the one who organizes, whether it is holding block meetings, supervising and assisting in keeping the neighbourhood clean from garbage, whether the garbage is litter or the drug dealer or pushers, the drug users (getting them help), on getting rid of muggers, the pimps and any other form of garbage.

He should strive to live up to his name by encouraging sisters, brothers, fathers, mothers and all Afrikans to nurture whatever skills they may have, teach them to open their own businesses, even if it's just a table at some programs that cater for Vendors, even if it is only in their spare time, on operating from, or renting a building, an Online store, writing good books, lecturing, operating a table or two at the Flea Market on weekends, etc.,

He should live up to his proud Afrikan name by encouraging Afrikan people to pool their resources to purchase buildings for residential and commercial purposes, you see many Afrikans have been lost in history because of their names, and this wasn't an accident it was the deliberate, premeditated, planned, design of the European slave master, so even today there are still debates about whether so and so, is or was European and that's all because of the names that Afrikan brothers and sisters carried , so Afrikan names should be reclaimed in order not only to take your place in history, but rightfully get the credit you deserve.

So reclaiming your names are not only important, but very important, and last but not least why propagate names that were forced on our ancestors, when we can reclaim our rightful names and proudly propagate them? You see what I mean.

CHAPTER 5

RECLAIMING OUR NAMES HELP US TO RECLAIM OUR IDENTITY

Reclaiming your names, is a great part of reclaiming your identity, as you begin to identify with your people, by reclaiming your names.

You have to continue further than just reclaiming your names, you have to find out who you are, where you came from, where you are, and where you are going.

You have to find out who you are, who are you?

Are you just the descendants of slaves?

Are you really a people with a history 400 years old that began with slavery and ended with it?

Are you a people without a sense of direction?

Are you a people accustomed to broken undisciplined homes?

Are you crude people wandering aimlessly?

Are you misdirected people?

Are you doomed to continue this way?

The answer, to all those questions, is a big NO!

We are not just the descendants of slaves, as our history goes beyond slavery, Afrikans visited the Western Hemisphere long before slavery, they came to North, Central, and South America, the Caribbean, and other parts of the Western World, this is easily proven in books written by professor Yosef ben Jochanan, Van Sertima, J. Hendrik Clarke, Chancellor Williams, Eric Williams etc., so we are not just descendants of slaves, some of these very slaves were kings, princes, queens, princesses, doctors, architects, surgeons, artists, singers, warriors etc.

Then there are those who were colonized in Afrika and still hold onto those foreign names (European).

Our history is not 400 years old, as some people will try to make you believe as we had vast Empires SONGHAI, MALI, EGYPT, NUBIA, AETHIOPIA, SUDAN, ETC., all ruled by AFRIKANS, all were really progressive, well organized civilizations, as they were ruled and organized by highly civilized people, not barbarians or cavemen.

We were a people with a sane, positive sense of direction, as these civilizations were almost totally free from crime, no unnatural behavior, no mass adulterous behaviour, no promiscuity, or prostitution houses, you see what I mean.

We were not people accustomed to broken homes, undisciplined children, we were not accustomed to abandoning our children or elders.

In Afrika there were no such institutions as the orphan home, or home for the aged etc., when both parents of any child or children died, they were immediately absorbed into the extended family, no orphan home, no adoption agency etc., when our fathers, mothers, aunts, uncles, got old, they were not herded into the homes for the aged or geriatric homes etc., they instead had a part to continue to play, instead of just presiding over their own immediate family, they now had a bigger role to play to train the young girls to be women, to be mothers, to be wives, to take care of the home etc.

The old men taught the young boys to be men, to be fathers, to be husbands, to take care of their wives, children and their homes, to be warriors, doctors, craftsmen etc. to lead well disciplined, productive lives.

We were not a crude people wandering aimlessly, our culture was well disciplined, crime was almost non-existent, there were no juvenile delinquents, as everyday was occupied constructively from the Cradle to the grave, no hanging out on the streets, no idling, no drug addicts, no pimps, no drug dealers, you see what I mean.

We were not a misdirected people as our sense of direction was good and even in the misdirected societies of this modern age , we still have many well-directed Afrikan leaders and teachers who are not going with the tide, if you fail to take hold of your mind, your mind would be taken over by the mass misdirection levelled at us, we would continue to see black-on-black crimes, black dope dealers, pushers and addicts, black fighting blacks etc. we, as Afrikan people must not follow the crowd, we must start by purging ourselves, stop hating ourselves, learn to love ourselves, start to Love Yourself and that love will flow out, the drug-dealing would stop, the drug selling would stop, the drug addiction would stop, why destroy our own people, a black on black crime is just as bad or even worse than any other crime, you must condemn and do something positive about crimes committed by our own, on our own, this must stop.

Parents you set the example, so that your children would have someone to emulate, not the trash on TV or the cinemas, but real life examples FATHER, MOTHER, OUR PROFESSORS, TEACHERS, SPORTSMEN E T C.,

You must realise that you are not just John Thomas on Henry James, you must realise that you came from a long line of honourable, great, intelligent people, a people with a long history of culture, civilization, greatness, progressive, understanding, intelligent, loving, caring, just, compassionate, constructive, free and freedom loving, you must Identify with such a people, your people, in fact YOURSELF.

The process must begin somewhere, and that somewhere is here, now, with Yourself, don't hold onto those European names, you have the freedom guaranteed under the Constitution of the United States of America, the Constitution of the United Kingdom, all the countries in the Caribbean and many countries of the world to change your names, this can be done legally at a very low cost you shop around for the conscious legal authority who would do it, not so much to make money, but for the upliftment of the Afrikan, the Afrikan race and Afrika.

Yes reclaiming your name helps you to reclaim your dignity, you try it.

CHAPTER 6

RECLAIMING OUR NAMES CAN HELP US TO RECLAIM OUR DIGNITY

You may ask how can I or we as a people reclaim our dignity in a crime ridden, destructive society such as we live in, the answer lies in "TRUTH".

You may ask how can "TRUTH" be the answer, okay, if you tell your children that smoking cigarettes, cigars, bidi, marijuana and drinking alcohol are wrong, but you smoke and drink, they would see that you are living a lie.

But if you don't smoke and don't drink alcohol, there they have a living example of how to live truthfully.

Some people force religion down their children's throats and they don't actively practice any religion. I am a Muslim, I pray every day, I read the Holy Quran every day, I try to live righteously everyday, I have submitted my will to Allah, I try my best to practice Allah's Divine System of Right Guidance, which is better than ritually following some religion, as it guides us to the right attitude towards our Creator and how to interact with our fellow humans, and even kindness towards animals and other species.

I don't force my belief on my children, but they have me as their example, I thank Allah that none of my children are on drugs etc.,

You must clean up yourself before you try to clean up others. You must place value on yourself, young men don't pull at the young women, get off the streets, read a good book, do some work among your friends. Show them how to live righteously, don't hang out on the street corner, be active in some kind of sports, martial arts, boxing, basketball, bodybuilding etc., get into some health building programs, you will be an inspiration to those your age, the younger ones and even the older ones, you see what I mean.

Ancient Afrika has many good things that the government in the West should put into practice, if they want an Ideal Society. As any Ideal Society must be based on TRUTH AND JUSTICE and that means putting everything in the right perspective, we must all love, respect and submit to the Almighty Creator and everything else would just fall in, we must be just in dealing with our fellow men, we must be just to our wives, the wives to their husbands, the parents to their children, the children to their parents, the young ones to the elders in general and then our governments must be just to the people, not favouring one ethnic group over the others as this is the ideal recipe for disaster as is presently proving each and every day.

Yes, we must reclaim our dignity and reclaim it now, we were the leaders and the examples for the entire world, you must reclaim that rightful position now!

Yes reclaiming your names would be the first step, you would not be "just a descendant of slaves" but rather the descendant of a proud, civilized people, a people who were law-abiding, a people who had righteous government, by the people for the people, a people whose fathers and mothers also looked after the extended family, as every child in the Afrikan civilization was an extension of the family, every adult was respected as an elder and oldest ones as examples for all, so reclaiming your names would add you to the long list of dignified progressive Afrikans in "Our Story which included Imhotep, Tutankhamon, Taharaka, Mansa Musa, Gebel Tarik, Menelik, Shaka Zula, Nzingha, Mpezeni, Cleopatra, Nefertiti etc.

CHAPTER 7

OUR HISTORY IS WRAPPED UP IN OUR NAMES

The biggest step in reclaiming your names, identity and dignity is AFRIKA, you might ask why, you may reason that I live in the U.S.A. I live in the Caribbean, I live in England, how can Afrika be the most important or biggest step why?

let us go back a little into the past, then we will return to the present, say let's go back past slavery, all our ancestors were living in AFRIKA, no problem then they had no problems of identity, they were AFRIKANS, now let's come forward a little, at the time of the slave trade, some of our ancestors were shipped to North American, the Caribbean, South America Europe etc.

Still at this point (the beginning) there were no problems of identity, they were just AFRIKANS, let's go forwarda little more, now the slave masters decide to take away the AFRIKANS' NAMES forcefully, he brutalizes them to accept the European names, remember when they were torn from their homeland, they had AFRIKAN NAMES, up to the point when they were forcefully made to abandon their original names, they still had AFRIKAN NAMES, now let us deviate briefly, as this is the right time to bring home this point, if as some AFRIKANS claim, a name or names are not so important, why didn't the slave masters leave them with their original names, this is a question for you to answer honestly in your own mind?

However, they (the slave masters) had a two-fold plan

Part 1: Their names would live on and be perpetuated by the Afrikans in the future, as is seen right now, every John Thomas every Shirley Jones, every Craig James would be a victory for them, a post slavery (physical) victory, it would be the confusion of the century.

Part 2: With the perpetuation of the European names, would also be their culture, their standards, their forms of everything and with that the DESTRUCTION OF AFRIKAN CIVILIZATION.

Now let us get back on track, now, even though force was used to change your names, a lot of the names still survived slavery and in the West we still have names like Kojo, Cudjoe, Cudjo, Qwamina etc., you might say that some Afrikans in Afrika have European names mixed with their names, but please remember that some were also enslaved and colonized on the continent of Afrika.

Now here is where Afrika becomes the uniting force, right now.

If you say for argument sake you want to identify with the present European names you are called by, who would be your famous personalities, what historical significance can a name like FITZROY CAMPBELL, AUDREY, CELIA, would you trace your ancestry to which European people? Are their historical examples of the past, your examples also, are their history yours? The answer is NO?

I had an encounter with an Afrikan woman with European names, it was at a Government Office, she asked me the meaning of my names, which I gladly gave to her, then I asked her names, which she told me, I then asked her the meaning of her names, she replied, "I don't know."

So why did she find it strange that an Afrikan man (myself) should have Afrikan names? What is so surprising or astounding about that? I knew the meaning of my names, but she didn't know the meaning of her (European) names.

When we have Afrikan names, say you name your son Shaka, you not only tell him the meaning of the name Shaka, but you can also tell him that he bears the name of a great Afrikan King who had the same name.

If you call your daughter Nzingha or Amina, you can tell her that Queen Nzingha fought for the liberation of Angola from European colonization, you can tell her that Queen Amina was so brave, was such a great ruler and warrior that she was often praised for her military achievements and rulership.

If you can call your son Imhotep, you can explain to him, that he was a genius not only in architecture, but he was the real "Father of Medicine", as he lived over 2,000 years before Hippocrates the so-called father of medicine, you see what I mean, names are important, look at the history connected to the names, directly and indirectly, think about it, don't name your children John Wayne and Burt Lancaster what significance could that have for our children, you see what I mean.

CHAPTER 8

WE MUST TEACH OUR CHILDREN TO LOVE THEMSELVES WE MUST TEACH THEM ABOUT OUR GREAT MEN AND WOMEN

So much self-hate and low self-esteem are taught to Afrikan children DELIBERATELY and OPENLY, that you have to combat that vigorously, look at the television cartoons, the shows, black people are almost always portrayed as comedians, brainless, careless, disorganised etc.

Our children are deceptively being taught to idolize, imitate and accept leadership from Europeans, they are being taught European standards, norms, behaviours etc.

Look at the comic books that an older generation of Afrikan children (now parents and grandparents) were brainstuffed on PHANTOM, MANDRAKE, SUPERMAN, BATMAN, TARZAN, DICK TRACY ETC. let's take a brief look and the absurdity of these super (?) entities.

PHANTOM

His forefather (grandfather or great-grandfather whatever) was left for dead and pygmies in Afrika rescued him, nursed him back to health and presto from then on, he and his ancestors automatically became the Peacemakers, the Protectors, the Guides, the Guardians of the great treasure in the cave, so the Rescuers (the pygmies) are now the servants, and the poor, almost dead European, has not only regained his health, but has amassed a great fortune, where did he get it from?

Regardless of the storyline the lesson to be learned is that these people cannot be trusted, as the rescuers are now the slaves.

MANDRAKE THE MAGICIAN

Could you imagine Mandrake the magician has a big strong PRINCE OF AFRIKA (LOTHAR) running behind him, and kicking down doors and beating up people for Mandrake, you see the absurdity of this story, Lothar prefers to be Mandrake's Hitman, instead of being a prince in Afrika, the subtle part is that Lothar might be hypnotised by Mandrake himself, you see what I mean.

SUPERMAN

He is an orphan from the planet Krypton, but note he has all European features, so that he could fit into American Society and not be identified as an alien, but say someone who is a Mexican right on the Southern border of the United State of America is considered as an alien, even in the comics, but Superman coming all the way from Krypton in another galaxy is all American, you see what I mean, he is even more American than the native Red Indians, why couldn't Superman be brown-skinned or black, according to the storylines, Krypton was a Hotter planet, than planet Earth, so why did Superman have to be white, he solves all the problems, he fights the bad guys, he stopped the train out of control, he rescues a plane that almost crashed, he fights the Communists etc., so when children are fed this garbage, they're indoctrinated to accept the SUPERIORITY (?) OF THE WHITE RACE..

BATMAN AND DICK TRACY

They are the best crime fighters in their localities, are there no black top crime fighters in their localities, why must Batman or Dick Tracy solve all the crimes in their areas, are black people in their localities dumb or weak so that they can't do the job? You see what I mean. Please note, originally when I wrote this book, the Superheroes were white, since then there are a lot of Black Superheroes, they make money for whoever write those stories. I rather go for real Great Afrikans such as Nzingha, Shaka, Imhotep, Amina, Mansa Musa, Gebel Tarik, Nkrumah, Jomo Kenyatta, Mandela etc.,

TARZAN

According to the story, the Apes reared Tarzan in Afrika, now we had so many Afrikan Civilizations, with Afrikans rearing their children to manhood and womanhood, teaching them all that they knew, how to live, how to fight, how to be just, how to be fair, how to rule, how to build houses, they educated them etc., but look at this with all the Education and Culture, no Afrikan man, woman or child regardless of how brave he or she was, no comic book writer even call any Afrikan "Lord of the Jungle:", but Tarzan, illiterate and brought up by the Apes is proclaimed "Lord of the Jungle" don't let them fool you with any savage talk as when they say "Lord of the Jungle" they mean "RULER OF THE JUNGLE (AFRIKA)" "KING OF THE JUNGLE (AFRIKA)" look at the Tarzan comics and movies, Tarzan is always killing black people, and intervening to bring peace among warring tribes, if that was really true, by the time Tarzan came on the scene, black people would have killed one another into extinction. You see what I mean

So we must educate our children to love black, let them know that all those white comic characters are just FICTION (LIES) let them know that we have real examples, some from the past and some living right in the present, tell your children about IMHOTEP, HANNIBAL, TAHARKA, TAARIK,

GENERAL GANGES, SHAKA, MPEZENI, MENELIK 1 & 2, TUTANKHAMUN, CRISPUS ATTUCKS, DENMARK VESSEY, OLAUDAH EQUIANO, DAAGA, NKRUMAH, ERIC WILLIAMS, MAURICE BISHOP, MANDELA, MALCOLM X, (AL HAAJ MALIK SHABAAZ), BOOKER T. WASHINGTON, FREDRICK DOUGLASS, QUEEN AMINA, QUEEN NZINGHA QUEEN NEFERTITI, HARRIETT TUBMAN ,MARY BETHUNE MCLEOD, ETC.

Teach them OUR STORY not His story

Instead of feeding your children with all the garbage, get good books (golden legacy) with our own great men and women, many DEAD AND LIVING EXAMPLES, so that they would know where they came from, where they are, and where they are going, don't let your children hang out on the block or the streets, as in slavery days any Afrikan who went to hang out, didn't return alive, don't even use that term HANGING OUT. Teach them to utilize their spare time constructively, let them read a good book, encourage them to participate in sports whether it be MARTIAL ARTS, BOXING, FOOTBALL, BASEBALL, SOCCER, ATHLETICS, SWIMMING, BASKETBALL, BODYBUILDING, ETC.

Encourage them to play chess, checkers, (Draughts) or any other sensible board games, they will place value on their time, show them that they could invest in a home based business, and save some money earned from it, show them to occupy their weekends, gainfully, instead of in crime or just wasting time, teach them real values, teach them that the real "YOU" is not the one in a pair of $500.00 sneakers or some expensive name brand jeans or shirt, show them that the real you, is the real you in a moderate priced apparel and shoes, show them not to waste , if they buy new clothes, don't throw away the old ones, give them to someone less privileged, or donate them to some needy fund, don't just throw them in the garbage, you noticed I said "SHOW, SHOW, SHOW, you get involved, find time for your children or else they may end up serving time.

Don't waste time telling your children about Santa Claus, you and I know that no white man is going to fill any bag with goodies and come down your chimney (even some houses without chimneys) to bring anything for your children, you let your children know that that's a lot of hog wash.

That season is kept alive for two reasons

1. To keep you in darkness religiously
2. To squeeze every dime out of your pocket and have you singing as you do so.

But have you ever noticed, that Santa comes to houses with a full bag and leaves with a full bag, it's the same old story, the slave masters came to Afrika with a ship full of garbage and left with a ship full of Doctors, Scientist, Architects, Teachers, Musicians, Agriculturist, Athletes etc., maybe Santa is doing the same thing in a different way.

CHAPTER 9

BEAUTIFUL, MEANINGFUL AFRIKAN NAMES

"Beautiful, Meaningful Afrikan Names", the title of this chapter speaks with power and authority. "Beautiful", Yes, Afrikan names are beautiful, not only by their sounds, but the Richness, Clarity and Dignity of the names.

"Meaningful", the meanings of the names give you the guidance in choosing proper names for you and your children.

Quoting from a previous chapter in this book, such dreadful meaning should be disowned by the Afrikan in favour of his (Afrikan) names. Check out these dread meanings.

Dolores, Delores	Sorrows/Sorrowful/Pain/Aches
Gladys	Welsh variant of Claudia, meaning Lame.
Celia, Cecilia	One of the meanings is Blind.
Cecil, Cicely	The meaning is Blind (From the Roman Clan name Caecilius)
Cecile	Feminine form of Cecil, which is derived from Caecilius, an old Roman family name, which has its root in the Latin caecus (blind, dim-sighted)

Claude is a relatively common French name for males originating from the Latin name Claudius, itself deriving from Claudicatio meaning "limping" or "stuttering" (Source :Wikipedia.org)

Claudia is the Latin feminine form of a prominent ancient Roman family name "claudus" meaning 'lame, crippled'. George means farmer.

So when you give your children worthwhile Afrikan names, you gain rather than lose, as their names would really be meaningful.

HOW SHOULD NAMES BE GIVEN

Names should never be chosen by only their sound, rather their meanings must be given first thought.

In the West, where so much of our tradition is lost, we must pick up the pieces and move on.

You should give your child his or her name at eight days old. The names chosen should then be given, if a child was born during a certain period e.g., prosperity, happiness, joy etc., one of the names chosen can be given to remember that time.

You must read over all the names carefully before selection. A guide is given regarding the pronunciation.

Remember, naming a child is a very serious matter, as this is what the child would be identified by.

This book "Afrikan Reclaim your Names, Identity and Dignity", gives details as to the importance of your Afrikan Names.

KEY TO PRONUNCIATION.

A   AH

BA   BAH

E   AY or EH. Example ME – MAY

I   EE Example, OLATUNGI – OH LAH TOON JEE

U   OO Example, TUNGI – TOON JEE

Traditionally, a name is given to the child for the day he or she was born. Examples are:

DAY	MALE	FEMALE	MEANING
Sunday	KWASI KWESI AKWASI	AKOSUA ESI	Under the Sun
Monday	KWADWO KOJO KODJOE	ADWOA ADJUA	Happy Humorous
Tuesday	KWABENA KOBINA	ABENAA ABINA	Peace
Wednesday	KWAKU	AKUA EKUA	Fame
Thursday	YAM YAU KWAW	YAA	Strength
Friday	KOFI	AFUA EFUA	Growth
Saturday	KWAME	AMA AMBA	Most Ancient

Remember, any Afrikan without Afrikan names is an anonymous, or missing person

MALE AFRIKAN NAMES

ABASI	Stern
ABEDE	Blessed Man
ABOLADE	He comes with Royalty
ABAYOMI	Ruler of People
ADANDE	Challenger
ADDAE	Morning Sun
ADE	Royal
ADENRELE	Crown Comes Home
ADELEKE	Crown on top
ADIGUN	Righteous
ADISA	One who makes himself Dear
ADEKOLA	Royal ties with the crown
ADEDOKUN	Crown's Glory Like Ocean
ADEBAYO	Crown meets Happiness
ADOFO	Warlike
ADEYEMI	My crown
ADEWALE	Crown Comes Home
AFIBA	By the Sea
AJAMU	He fights for what he wants
AJENE	true
AKIL	Intelligent
AKINI	Male Child or eldest male in the family
AKINOLA	Royalty is bravery
AKINTOLA	Bravery is Loyalty
AKINLANA	Valour is bravery
ALEMU	His World
ALUKO	Brother of peace
ALPHA	Leader
AMEGAH	A Big Man
ANDOM	He is their Pillar
ANYIKA	I am too strong for my Enemies
APATA	Rock
ANOKYE	Does not clear to catch
ASKARI	Warrior; Soldier

ATIBA	Understanding
ATO	Brilliant
AZIKIWE	Vigorous
B	
BABALOLA	Royalty is father of all
BABATUNDE	Father has Returned
BAKO	First Born
BABU	Chief
BALEWA	Happiness
BOBO	Born on Tuesday
BANDELE	Born away from Home
BOMANI	Warlike
BANKOLE	Help me to build this House
BARUTI	Teacher
BWERANI	You are welcome
BAYE	Father
BEKABANTU	Look after the people
BEKITEMBA	Trust
C	
CAZEMBE	Wiseman
CHAKUMBA	Born away from Home
CHANGA	Strong like iron
CHINYELU	One who is invincible
CHUMA	Wealth
CHICA	Beloved
CHUI	An Aggressive person
CHIDUKU	The little one
COMLAN	Born on Friday
CHIKUYO	A man who is cultured
CHIUMBO	Small Creation
CHIWALE	Handsome
CHIONESU	Guiding light
CHINAMANO	The sensible one

D

DAMANY	Thoughtful
DEDAN	Town Dweller
DELA	Saviour
DIA	Champion
DIKE	Brave and warlike
DINGANE	A person in need
DIALLO	Bold
DIN	Great
DIALLOBE	Heroic
DIOP	Ruler
DUGUMA	Spear
DOMELEVO	Don't take people for their face value
DUNDUZA	Man of adventure
DWAMINA	Clearer of way, courageous
DZIGBODI	Patience
DZWORNU	Courage
DZODZOME	Nature

E

EDU	Tenth Born
ENAHORO	Like the sun
ERASTO	Man of peace
ESAN	Reward

F

FARAI	Let us Rejoice
FELA	warlike
FODAIBA	Craftsman
FOLI	Tall

G

GAMBA	Warrior
GIRMA	Glory
GOGO	Like GrandFather
GORA	Hero

GONDO	Eagle
GOREDEMA	Black Cloud
GOWON	Rainmaker
GUILA	Dark Stranger

H

HAGOS	Joy
HONDO	Warrior

I

IDOWU	Famous
IFOMA	Lasting friend
IMO	Knowledge
IRUNGU	One who puts things in order
IREGI	Revolter
ITALO	Full of valour, very brave

J

JABARI	A brave Person
JABULANI	Be happy
JARAMOGI	A brave person
JAWARA	Peace loving
JAWANZA	Dependable
JEGEDE	Easy going child
JELANI	Mighty
JOJO	Born on Monday

K

KAHERO	Conceived at home
KALA	Tall
KALAMO	The unexpected one
KAMAU	Quiet and warlike
KALONJI	Man of victory
KOFI	Growth
KWADWO	Happy
KAMBUI	Fearless
KANYAMA	Guard

KARAMO	Scholar
KAMARA	Teacher
KAMUZO	Medicinal
KAREGA	Rebel
KWAKU	Fame
KWABENA	Peace
KARANJA	Guide
KASHIKA	Friendly
KAYODE	He brought Joy
KEFENTSE	Conqueror
KEFIM	Black
KEFING	Black man
KENYATTA	Musician
KENYA	Artist
KIJANA	Young Fighter
KIAMBU	Rich
KIMANI	Sailor
KITAKA	Good Farmer
KONTAR	Only Child
KONATA	Man of high station
KOREDE	He brings good luck
KOKAYI	Summon the people
KOMUNYAKAA	Passionate
KWASI	Under the sun
KWAME	Most Ancient
KUMI	Forceful
KUNLE	The home is filled with honour
KIBWE	Blessed
KORO	Golden
KODJO	Humorous
KOUTO	He who struggles to live
KOPANO	Union

L

| LASANA | Poet |
| LESEDI | Light |

LUKATA	Dynamic
LUMUMBA	Gifted
LUMO	Born face downwards
LUTALO	Warlike

M

MABATANO	Togetherness
MACHARRIA	Lasting Friend
MADU	Man
MAKALANI	Skilled in writing
MAKESI	Brainy
MANANI	The beneficent One
MANU	Second born
MAKERE	Marvellous
MASIMBA	Power
MATSIMELA	Roots
MAVU	The earth
MAWUSI	In the hands of God
MAWUTO	God's own
MBITA	Born on a cold Night
MBWANA	Master
MENKA	Does not say
MLINZI	The protector
MODIBO	Helper
MOMBERA	Man of Adventure
MODEIRA	Teacher
MENSAH	Third Son
MOHENI	Lightning
MONDE	Patience
MORIBA	Curious
MONGO	Famous
MONTSHO	Black
MOSEGI	Tailor
MOSI	First born
MOYO	Well being, good health
MUATA	Searcher

MUDADA	The Provider
MUGABE	Athlete
MUGO	Man of Peace
MULIRO	Fire
MURIU	Unknown
MUTEMA	Black Man
MUTOPE	Protector
MUTSA	Kindness
MWAMBA	Strong
MWANDO	Good worker
MWANGI	Conqueror
MWANZA	Wise Protector
MWATA	Sensible
MZEE	Wise man

N

NABATE	Little
NANGWAYA	Don't trifle with me
NEGOMO	Mountain
NETFA	Free Man
NGUVU	Powerful and Strong
NEKORO	From Now onwards
NKU	Eye of God
NOGOMO	Prosperous
NONO	Scholar, Wise
N'NAMDI	Father's name lives on
N'NANNA	Grandfather
NSAMI	One who moves a lot
NOKWARE	Truth
NURU	Born during Daylight
NYAHUMA	Helper of Men
NYASHA	Sympathy
NYAWI	Black man

O

OBA	King
OBAFEMI	Tall
ODAI	Third Son
ODINGA	Wood carver
OGINGA	Drummer
OKPARA	First Son
OLUBUNMI	Lord gives me a Gift
OLADELE	Royalty reaches home
OLAYENI	Royalty benefits us
OLUWOLE	Lord visits my home
OMARI	Wise Man
OLA	Noble man
OLATUNDE	Royalty comes again
OLU	Highest among people
OMATOYO	The arrival of this baby brings Joy
OLUGBALA	Saviour of the people
OJI	Gift bearer
OLYVIA	Fire
OKON	Born at Night
OMOWALE	Son returns home
ONI	Born in a sacred place
OYEWOLE	Chieftain has come home

P

PILI	Second son
POPOOLA	The path to Honour

R

REKAYI	Leave alone
REMA	Revolt
RUDO	Love
RUNAKO	Handsome
RUVIMBO	Confidence

S

SANDO	Hammer (Powerful character)
SANGA	From the Valley
SAWANDI	The founder
SEITU	Artist
SEKOU	Fighter
SELE	Strong like an Elephant
SEVE	Aggressive
SHAKA	Beetle: Name of Great Afrikan Zulu King
SHONARI	Forceful
SHUMBA	Lion
SIPHO	Gift
SITHEMBISO	Promise
SIMBA	Strong like lion
SIMWENYI	One who smiles all the time
SOZUFE	Never dies
SONKONI	From the sea
SUDE	Luck
SULE	Adventurous

T

TACUMA	Alert
TAU	Lion (Born out of bravery)
TAYO	Mine is Joy
THEMBEKILE	Trustworthy
TESFA	Hope
TESFAYE	My hope
THABITI	A true man
THEMBA	Hope: to trust
THABO	Pleasure
TOJO	Story Teller
TOGBI	Grandpa
TOOLA	Workman
TUSO	Help

TSHAKA	Beetle: Name of Great Afrikan Zulu King
U	
UFA	Flower
UGO	Eagle
UMI	Life
UWEZO	Power
UZOMA	The right way
V	
VUKANI	Wakeup
VITA	War
W	
WIMANA	Belongs to God
WAMUKOTA	Left handed
Y	
YAMURO	Helper
YAHARA	Blessing
YAMEOGO	Wealthy
YAMRO	Courteous
YERO	Warrior
Z	
ZAMBO	Holy Prince
ZANELE	Enough
ZANO	Idea
ZANI	Ancient
ZINDOGA	One who solves His problems independently
ZWADE	Chosen leader

FEMALE AFRIKAN NAMES

A	
ADUKE	Chosen with love
AMINA	Trustful: peaceful one
ABA	Born on Thursday
ABEO	Come to bring happiness
ABAYOMI	Pleasant meeting
ADJUA	Born on Monday
AMBA	Born on Saturday
AYO	Joy
ABEBA	Flower
AYANA	Beautiful Flower
ASSITOU	Careful
AFRIYE	Has come at the right time
ADANNA	Fathers Daughter
ADE	The crown
AKWOKWO	Younger of Twins
ADERO	Life Giver
ADWOA	Happy
ADUNNI	A child that all will like to have
ABENAA	Peace
AYINKE	Beloved and praised
AKUA	Fame
ASHABI	She is chosen one in birth
ASHAKE	Adopted with love
AYODELE	Joy enters the home
ABIMBOLA	Born to be rich
AMMA	Famous
ABIOLA	Born into Honour
ADAMA	Queenly
AKWETE	Elder of Twins
ASHAKI	Beautiful
ASHA	Life
ADEBOLA	Glorious

ASATA	Warlike
ASANTEWAA	Warrior woman
ADESIMBO	Noble Birth
AINKA	The cherished one
AMA	Most Ancient

B

BAYO	Joy is found
BAMIDELE	Hope
BIRUNGI	Beautiful
BOLADE	Honour arrives
BOATEMAA	Helps to strengthen things
BUNMI	My gift

C

| CHINUE | Gods own blessing |

D

DADA	Having curly hair
DAMALI	Beautiful vision
DARA	Beautiful
DAYO	Joy arrives
DEKA	She who pleases

E

EFUA	Born on Friday
EKUA	Born on Wednesday
ESHE	Life
ESI	Born on Sunday
EWUNIKI	Fragrant
EZIGBO	Beloved
EBUN	Gift

F

FABU	Beautiful woman
FANTU	Beautiful Day
FOLAYAN	To walk in dignity

H

HEMBADOON	The winner

I

IFAMA	Everything is fine
IFETAYO	Love Brings happiness
IGE	Delivered feet first
IKANGA	Generous

K

KEMBA	Faithful
KINDA	Young beautiful Woman
KOBI	Go also
KUMIWA	Brave

L

LINDA	Wait
LOLONYO	Love is beautiful
LULU	Jewel

M

MANANA	Lustrous
MAWUSI	In the hands of God
MAYIMUNA	Expressive
MAKINI	Strength of character
MANDISA	Sweet
MAWAKANI	Yielding
MFON	Grace, gift
MODUPE	I thank God
MOBOLADE	Pleasant
MONIFA	I am lucky
MOTIRYO	Faithful
MOTISOLA	Understanding
MOTIRAYO	Fiery
MUBA	Fully satisfied
MUDIWA	Beloved one

MUGA	Mother of all
N	
NEGESTI	Queen
NDIBI	Patience
NGOZI	Blessing
NJOKI	Our daughter has returned home
NJERI	Anointed
NOBANTU	Loved by people
NWABATA	Active
NOMUSA	Kindness
NIMAAKO	Knows how to fight
NOYOLO	Peaceful
NYAKU	Child of wealth
NOZIBELE	Generous one
NYAAKO	Slow to fight
NSENGA	Womanly delight
NKENGE	Superior Mind
NGINAA	One who serves
NSOMBI	Abounding Joy
O	
OBIOMA	Kind hearted
ODE	Born along the road
OKOLO	Friendly
OKON	Born at night
OSEYE	The happy one
OMODELE	Blessed child comes home
OLA	Precious
OLABISI	Happiness
OSEGE	The happy one
OLUBAYO	The highest joy
OLUFEMI	God loves me
OMADARA	Wonderful child
OMOROSE	Beautiful child
OYIN	Honey

P	
PHILOMENA	Flower
PO	Knot
R	
RUDO	Love
S	
SADIO	Pure
SARA	Remain alone
SARAN	Joy
SALA	Gentle and loving
SERWA	Noble woman
SIGOLWIDE	My ways are straight
T	
TIA	Short
TITI	Flower
TOMBI	Lovely girl
U	
UZOMA	The right way
W	
WAMBUI	Singer of songs
WEYNI	Sweetest Desire
Y	
YAA	Strength
Z	
ZENZELE	Do it yourself
ZOLA	Quiet, productive
ZINGHA	Beautiful
ZWENA	Good

CHAPTER 10

CONCLUSION

After being deceived, conned, robbed, lied to, denied what was rightfully ours, took away our names by force, and violent force at that, then what is the setback in reclaiming our names, at least which we can do legally (according to their laws) and peacefully, why cling to those names some of which means lame, blind and stupid meanings, some are even disrespectful and degrading, what's the keep back?

You spend so much time and money celebrating meaningless holidays, which when you check their origins, they go against us, and not only that they are down right disrespectful to our intelligence, so why should we even respect these so-called holidays, why should we celebrate them?

Why not take that same money and invest it in changing your names, in fact reclaiming your true Afrikan names?

For more detailed information on these senseless holidays read my book THE PAGANISM IN SOME CHRISTIAN CHURCHES.

Show your children respect and they will respect you, never call them stupid, dumb or foolish, but rather you can say, "You are too intelligent to do something like that."

You try that and you'll see it makes a lot of difference, the next point I want to make, don't go with the crowd, as in most instances the crowds may be wrong, investigate, investigate, investigate, don't take anything with a pinch of salt, challenge anything, and get the answers, and don't take no for an answer.

Read, Read, Read, Read good books, not those trash, with black faces, instead of reading those cheap novels, where all they did was change the characters to black (also the authors), don't buy that stuff, there are too many good books around for you to read, so why waste time reading garbage, what goes into your head, through your eyes comes out through your mouth, if you read garbage, that's all you'll be talking about, you can't expect to read garbage and be able to intelligently talk about "BLACK HISTORY, OR HEALTH OR ANY INTELLIGENT SUBJECT," no it won't be possible, I have seen it all the time on the train, the bus, the airport, at terminals, black people reading all this garbage, I wonder if they have a serious famine for good books, or I ask myself if these people are inoculated against good books.

AFTERWORD

After reading so much about the way our names, spirituality and culture were taken from us, we need to stop and think, some of the names (European) which we have are meaningless, and some of us are living up to those worthless meanings.

As the saying goes "Charity begins at home", so lets start loving each other from home and let it spread abroad, to the neighbours, people we meet on the streets, in commuting, at the supermarket (and lets own our own supermarkets) at the laundromat, at the department stores etc., (Lets own our own businesses), instead of being hostile to each other be friendlier, lets exude love and kindness, as if you can't love your own self, who would you love, you can't hate yourself (your people) and love another, your love would be questionable, it can't be real.

And last but not least, don't let people brand you with misnomers, how can we be THIRD WORLD PEOPLE, WHEN OUR CIVILIZATION WAS FIRST.

OUR CULTURE WAS FIRST, OUR HISTORY WAS FIRST, OUR INVENTIONS WERE FIRST, OUR ACHIEVEMENTS WERE FIRST, THEREFORE WE ARE FIRST WORLD PEOPLE, AFRIKA WAS FIRST.

MORE BOOKS BY ABOLADE NKOSI TAYO

- ❖ AFRIKA! THE TRUE ORIGIN OF KARATE AND ALL MARTIAL ARTS

- ❖ SOME INTERESTING FACTS ABOUT AŞA KINIUN AFRIKAN MARTIAL ARTS

- ❖ HOW TO TAKE CONTROL OF YOUR MIND

- ❖ CARIBBEAN FOLKTALES

- ❖ JINN, GHOST OR NATURAL PHENOMENA - WHICH?

- ❖ REINCARNATION OR MEMORY TRANSFER - WHICH?

- ❖ SCIENCE GONE MAD

- ❖ SIMPLE NUTRITION

- ❖ DISTURBING CONSEQUENCES.

To order go to www.lulu.com/spotlight/nkosi2020